the MODERN MAMIL

HOW TO LOOK PRO

ICE HOUSE BOOKS

Published by Ice House Books

Illustrations copyright © 2019 Spencer Wilson
Text copyright © 2019 Ice House Books

Concept, illustration and design by Spencer Wilson
courtesy of Yellow House Art Licensing www.yellowhouseartlicensing.com

Written by Chris McGuire
Edited by Samantha Rigby

Ice House Books is an imprint of Half Moon Bay Limited
The Ice House, 124 Walcot Street, Bath, BA1 5BG
www.icehousebooks.co.uk

ISBN 978-1-912867-09-7

Printed in China

WELCOME MAMILS

Congratulations on obtaining this invaluable guide.

Like all Middle Aged Men In Lycra, you know in your heart of hearts that, if there was any justice in the world, you'd be a pro-cyclist. If only the stars had aligned differently, making you taller, thinner, sportier or less fond of cake – it all could have been so different. You'd have been up there on the podium with the trophies, the sponsorship deals and the press intrusion.

Never fear, you may not BE a pro, but that doesn't mean you can't LOOK like one. The book you're holding right now is the key to looking the part. From socks to shaving, cadences to coffee-shop culture, we cover it all.

Trust us, after reading this guide, you won't be able to go out for a spin without someone shouting: "There goes a total pro!"

You can thank us later.

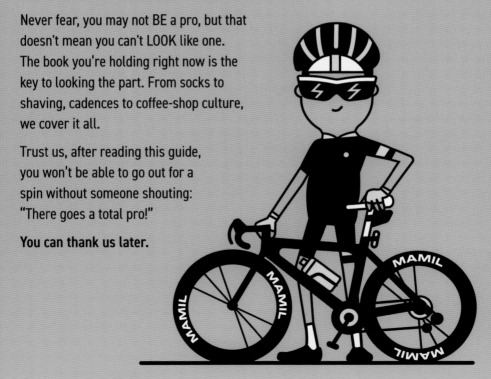

SECTION ONE

PRE-RIDE
PREPARING TO LOOK PRO

SLAM THE

Simply put, this means to have the handle bars as low as they'll go.

Pros 'slam the stem' because it makes them very 'aero'.

Aero is an abbreviation of the word 'aerodynamic'. Pros shave off the second part so they can say it faster. Using the word 'aero' as often as possible makes you sound hugely pro.

Note, eating Aero bars on a ride (even mint ones) doesn't make you look pro.

Riding in the 'slammed stem' position is likely to give you a bad back. So, if you're not a yoga master, it may be wise to keep two strong men standing by to lift you from your bike at the end of the ride.

If you can't see your feet while standing up, you shouldn't slam the stem.

SHAVE YOUR LEGS

If you want to get the pro look, you have to shave your legs. It's as simple as that.

There has been vigorous debate on why shaving is necessary. The main 'reasons' include – 'shaving makes a pro more aero' (that word again) to 'smooth legs help with post-ride massage'.

At the end of the day, it doesn't matter WHY you shave your legs. If you want the pro look, it's a necessity.

Ask a woman for help (someone you know, not just a random lady from the street). Also think about where you want to stop – if you shave to the knee and then wear swimming trunks, you risk the 'novelty hairy under-shorts' look.

There has been speculation that some men become MAMILs simply to have a legitimate excuse to shave their legs. This is, of course, untrue.

SHAVE YOUR ARMS?

This is extreme. And only for those who REALLY want to look pro.

Yes, you'll be slightly more 'aero', but you're never going to be quick enough for it to count. Sometimes the truth hurts.

Only shave your arms if you want to go for the ultimate win over your MAMIL mates.

WARNING: Keep a steady hand. Shaving cuts on your legs can be embarrassing, but going out with bits of bloody tissue peppering your arms looks down-right ridiculous – and very un-pro.

<u>DON'T</u> SHAVE YOUR BITS

There is no need whatsoever to shave your bits in order to look pro. Frankly, if people can see you're unshaven down below, you need to consider a new pair of shorts.

If you shave your bits but not your beard or head, you can't use the 'aero' argument as an excuse. Just sayin'.

DON'T BE A SH*T KIT MISFIT

Here's where things get tricky.

Achieving the pro look with your kit is a real balancing act.

Why? Because looking like a pro doesn't mean dressing like one.

Firstly, don't buy team replica kits. It's just not done. You risk being labelled a 'full-kit w*nker', which is ironic as it's difficult to imagine any clothing that gives you less easy access to your bits.

Secondly, do some research (a quick Google) and find out what your favourite pro wears in training. A training kit is perfect for that pro look. Don't wear more than two brands at once, and stick to black.

Remember, nothing looks more amateurish than a Tour De France yellow jersey or the rainbow stripes of a winner – unless you've actually earned them (which raises the question, why are you reading this?).

Always strategically place one item of damaged (yet high-quality) kit in your ensemble. This will show you're too far into the pro-zone to worry about kit damage.

Finally, nobody ever achieved the pro look without perfect bib shorts. If your shorts don't sit like a second skin, nothing else you do will matter. Sagging gussets are a no-no. Also, be sure to check your luggage is appropriately positioned and not playing peekaboo over the pad. Here endeth the lesson.

WARNING: Never wear damaged shorts, this could lead to all manner of unwanted consequences. The only thing worse than a drooping gusset is a holey one.

SOCKS APPEAL

As any true MAMIL knows, cyclists (especially pros) get quite wound up about socks. Bless them.

To look properly pro, make sure your socks are white and rise to exactly six inches above the ankle.

Many pros, it is said, would rather stay at home than wear the wrong socks on the bike.

Consider taking a tape measure with you on every ride, to ensure your socks are always at the right height. Remember, men can often be confused about how long six inches really is.

WARNING: Never store the tape measure down your shorts. A misfiring spring-loaded unit could do immeasurable damage to your heirlooms.

NEVER
TOO HIGH
JUST RIGHT
TOO LOW

BO SELECTA!

Warming up on a turbo trainer before a race is a VERY pro thing to do.

You'll often see the pros, tops unzipped, working up a comfortable sweat on their turbo trainer as they take final team instructions – it's the cycling equivalent of an orchestra tuning up for a performance (just with slightly more Lycra).

Why not bring a turbo trainer to your next sportive? Set it up next to your car, don your headphones and get into the zone while listening to your ultimate warm up playlist (NB: if this doesn't include *Eye Of The Tiger* something is very wrong somewhere). Trust us, you'll look like a HUGE pro.

Why not warm down after the sportive on your turbo trainer too? You'll look just like Chris Froome. OK, not 'just like' him (unless you actually do look like him), but you'll look pretty darn pro.

Remember, rain won't help your turbo trainer sessions, so always have a member of your team standing by to protect you with an umbrella.

WARNING: It's possible that warming-up (and down) on a turbo trainer before (and after) your local sportive won't do anything for your popularity with the other cyclists. Yes, you'll look like a TOTAL pro, but there's a small chance people will point and laugh.

06 LAY IT

ON THICK

It's very easy to get cold on the bike in Lycra. **RIDICULOUSLY COLD.**

Colder than a snowman's frosty bits....

You get the idea.

Make sure you're dressed for the weather! Riding in the wrong kit for the conditions is a very un-pro thing to do.

Layering up is the key to beating the cold weather. Essentially, wear every bit of kit you own all at once.

Keep the cheap stuff out of sight. Use Aldi kit as a base-layer with Rapha on top, NEVER the other way round.

WARNING: Wearing many layers of kit will slow you down if you need to pee. Plan for this, or things could get warm and soggy very quickly.

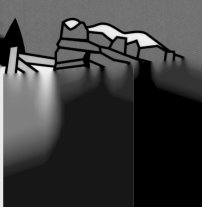

SECTION TWO

THE RIDE
LOOKING PRO IN THE SADDLE

EASY RIDER

Pros make riding a bike in the peloton seem easy. They take on the Alpe d'Huez in 30-degree heat (chased by a fan in a chicken suit) and it looks like a walk in the park. It isn't.

Any MAMIL wanting to be mistaken for a pro must make cycling seem as natural as breathing. Even if you're hating every moment of your ride, keep up a confident grin and you'll appear EXTREMELY pro. If you fall off your ride, act like that's exactly what you meant to do. Sunglasses help – they hide those tears of pain and frustration.

WARNING: Sometimes pros totally lose the plot, often after a major mechanical. So, on certain occasions, it's true to say that throwing a bike into a verge does look VERY pro. But we take no responsibility for any loss of limb or Lycra that may result from acting in this way.

THE GLANCE

When cycling, it's essential to regularly check what's happening behind you.

How this is done (most bikes aren't fitted with rear-view mirrors) highlights the difference between a regular MAMIL and a total pro.

Simply turning your head and looking over your shoulder sends signals to those 'in the know' that you're a commuter – and not a possible yellow-jersey wearer. The method preferred by the pros, in order to stay as aero as possible, is to take a glance under the armpit.

Some MAMILs tend to sweat (lots), so this armpit-glance technique, although pro in appearance, may not be for them. If sweating is an issue, we'd advise continuing to look over your shoulder. Glancing under your armpit may be a little like peering into the Niagara Falls.

WARNING: Perfecting the armpit-glance method of hindsight isn't easy. It takes practice, lots of practice. Consider doing it at slow speeds first. Perhaps road-test the technique while walking – although be prepared to glimpse some funny looks (via your pit).

09

THE SPIN CYCLE

'Cadence' isn't just a posh girls' name – it's something everyone who wants to look pro should know about. Put simply, it's the number of times the pedal crank spins per minute.

Chris Froome is famed for a high-cadence climbing technique. Using low gears, Froome pedals at a very high rate, helping him power up the long ascents of the grand tours. Copying Froome (developing a consistently high cadence on climbs) would make you look very pro indeed.

However, we'd recommend you don't experiment with cadence levels in public straight away. Do it on your turbo trainer at home first. That way, nobody will be around to see how exhausted you are after five minutes.

WARNING: Attempting to spin at cadence rates similar to Froome's is a risky strategy and TOTALLY exhausting. If you hit a climb and stick your ride into the 'granny gear' straight away, you're far more likely to cramp up than go up!

BE A CORNER PERFORMER

There's no doubt that getting low (ridiculously close to the asphalt) when you take a corner looks very pro. To put it bluntly, if you can't grab a slice of pizza from the tarmac (with your teeth) as you corner, you're probably not low enough.

That said, there's a very fine line between getting close to the road and crashing into it. The skill in cornering isn't just about leaning into a curve, it's also about getting vertical again.

WARNING: For most mere mortals, attempting to corner like a pro will end up in a trip to the local A&E department. Skidding (at speed) along tarmac is likely to make a large hole in any Lycra you're wearing, and it'll have a similar effect on your skin. Not to mention, overshooting a corner and coming face-to-face with an oncoming lorry has a habit of not ending well.

On the plus side, getting back on the saddle in tattered kit that shows off freshly acquired wounds is a VERY pro look. To be fair, being stretchered off to hospital looks pretty pro, too.

GET 'THE LOOK'

In 2001, cycling history was made when a pro (who shall remain nameless) cracked Jan Ullrich on the Alpe d'Huez. After appearing to struggle, the pro suddenly took the lead, looked over his shoulder and coolly caught Ullrich's eye, staring him out before accelerating away and breaking Ullrich's team morale. This ultimate throw of shade will forever be known as 'The Look'.

There's no doubt that copying 'The Look' is a very pro thing to do. Essentially, you need to make eye contact with another rider, just at the point where you speed away from them. Why not practise in front of a mirror at home? We'd recommend you do this when everyone else is out – or you might be the recipient of some strange looks yourself.

WARNING: Before you try to execute 'The Look', make sure you can keep up the pace you're about to set. It's very un-pro to speed past riders only for them to overtake you a minute later – when you've passed out from exhaustion.

TEMPO

ZONE 2

12

WATT'S IT ALL ABOUT?

Any MAMIL would be wise to invest in a power meter. These devices show how many watts of energy you're putting through your bike. Using a meter for guidance, it's possible to adapt your ride to keep within particular levels of exertion: known as zone 1, zone 2, etc. Each of these zones has different benefits.

The trouble is, learning about the pros and cons of the zones is incredibly tedious. So why not forget about the detail? Instead, shout (as often as possible) that you're 'finding your sweet spot in zone 2!', 'keeping it tempo' or similar. Other riders will be convinced that you're a pro.

WARNING: Taking it the extra step and adding power to your ride in the form of a hidden motor is STRICTLY frowned upon in pro circles. 'Mechanical doping' may save your legs on inclines, but you're likely to be found out – especially if you forget to turn off the motor (when you stop en-route for a flat white) and your bike keeps going without you.

DON'T DODGE THE DRAFT

Drafting – benefitting from the break in air resistance caused by a vehicle or rider in front of you – is a very pro thing to do.

Riding in a 'chain gang' – a group of five or more cyclists taking it in turns to lead, allowing the rest to draft in their wake – is a great way to conserve energy. It also ensures you maintain high average speeds, so it looks great on your Strava record!

Drafting is all about teamwork. Any MAMIL who only takes the lead in downhill sections won't be popular with the rest. You'll develop a reputation and probably a pithy nickname to boot.

Remember, the drafting technique is only useful if someone fast or large is ahead of you. So, riding in the slipstream of a little fella, with stabilizers on his road bike, won't make you look pro, at all.

We'd advise examining your diet before drafting in close proximity with other MAMILs. Nobody wants to linger behind someone creating a fragrant 'draft' of their own. Get the picture?

WARNING: Never try and copy the pros by drafting behind a vehicle. Being scraped off the back of a lorry is a VERY un-pro look.

FLICK

Taking the lead in your group so others can draft behind you is EXHAUSTING.

After a few minutes you're far too knackered to speak, giving you the chance to do something hugely pro: FLICK YOUR ELBOW. This lets the others know it's their turn to pull to the front, while you take (a lot) of time to recover at the back.

Learning to do the elbow flick as ostentatiously as possible is essential for looking pro. You need to appear a total martyr as you fall to the back of the group, slump over your handlebars and sigh. In years to come, they'll write operas about your struggle today.

WARNING: There's no point in looking like a pro if there's nobody there to see you. Only lead the group when riding through densely populated areas, where there's a high chance you'll whizz past a dawdling social rider or commuter. Don't forget to show off by shouting every cycling phrase in your vocabulary as you pass.

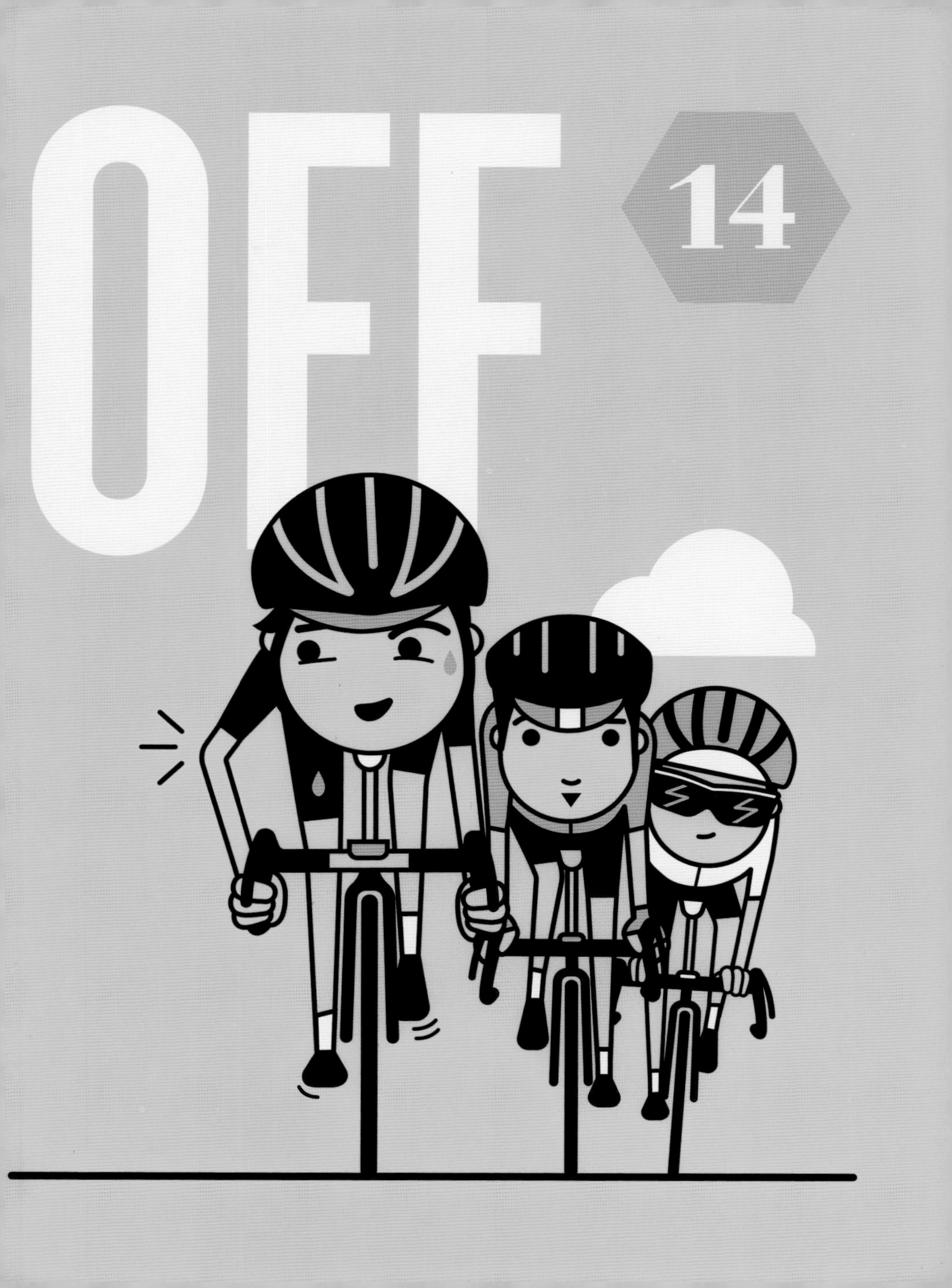
OFF
14

TO LEG IT!

MAMIL or pro, there's no getting away from it – holding position on the drops for long periods of time can make you stiff (so to speak).

But don't waste time stopping – learn to stretch your legs while you're still on the bike. Simply unclip and hook a foot over the saddle for a satisfyingly pro-looking hamstring/abductor stretch. You'll feel better – and look very pro indeed.

WARNING: Only do this if you have a great sense of balance. If you're one of those MAMILs who considers it an achievement to finish a ride without flying over the handlebars, don't bother! Stretching your leg, losing your balance and crashing into bushes is a VERY un-pro thing to do.

NB: For those 'in the know' this stretch will look HUGELY pro. Unfortunately, to everyone else it'll look like you're doing the cycling version of John Cleese's silly walk.

GIVE IT ALL THAT

When cycling in a group, the leading rider is expected to shout warnings and give hand signals about upcoming hazards.

Calling out 'slowing!' with an outstretched arm and slowly flapping your hand indicates the group should slow. Shouting 'hole!' and pointing out a pothole helps keep the group safe.

Yet, these calls don't make a rider look pro – they're basic stuff that any Sunday rider should know. To really set yourself apart, you'll need to up your shouts and signals game. Calls of 'inside', 'tempo' and 'full gas' – meaning 'don't cut me up', 'a controlled pace' and 'ride as hard as you can' – will take any MAMIL's calls to the pro level.

Equally, tapping the next rider on the bottom to let them know you're there is a gesture sure to earn you lots of pro kudos. That said, only do this if you know the rider well, otherwise it may result in a punch on the nose.

Remember, if it's 6am and you're speeding through a tiny hamlet, it's unlikely your bellowed calls of 'tempo' and 'GRAVEL! GRAVEL!' will do anything to make MAMILs more popular in the community at large.

Try practising your calls and signals before you get on the bike – lock yourself in the bathroom and recite some key peloton phrases. But only do this when everyone is out, as calls of 'HOLE!', 'INSIDE!' and 'SLOWING!' emanating from your loo might give the family cause for concern.

GET SOME STICKY

MAMILs love it when family show support for their cycling passion by joining them on a ride. But, if the sight of you in Lycra has put your clan off becoming mini-MAMILs, there's another way to get them involved.

Why not get your family to run a TEAM CAR for you?

We're serious. Get your kids to help with some 'sticky bottle' assistance. This trick (requesting a drink from the support car, then holding onto the sticky bidon as it's passed to you) allows MAMILs to be towed for a short period, conserving their energy. A VERY pro move!

WARNING: There's a small chance your partner, who has been standing by you through thick and thin (mainly thick) since you became a MAMIL, may not react well to being asked to run a support car. We accept no responsibility for any repercussions (or divorce proceedings) that may occur as a result.

SUPPORT

THE WHEEL DEAL

From punctures to buckled hubs, wheels can (and will) make or break a ride. But it's not what happens to a wheel, but what the rider does to fix it that's important.

Any MAMIL heading out in full Lycra who doesn't know how to fix a puncture is liable to become a laughing stock. We recommend you practise mending a puncture in private, that way you'll be sorted when you're required to do it in public. It WILL happen.

If you want to take puncture repair to the next level, why not detach and hold up your wheel for a replacement? This will be the cue for your family (in the support car) to come to your aid. Do this and EVERYONE will think you're very pro indeed.

WARNING: A MAMIL who can't fix a puncture is just a man in tights.

HANDS UP!

Pros don't stop, even to pee, so learning
how to cycle hands-free is essential.

Being able to ride without your hands on the bars
is something that separates mere mortals from the gods (well, pros at least).
Eating, drinking and even changing clothes in the saddle, without holding the
handlebars, are all VERY pro looks. If you can pull off putting on a rain cape
without ending up in a hedge, you'll look VERY pro indeed.

WARNING: Any activity that involves taking your grip off the handlebars requires a huge
amount of balance and will, if not performed perfectly, end up in a crash. To put it bluntly,
if you're a fan of hospital food, this is the pro-look for you! With safety in mind, you could
perfect your hands-free tricks on a static bike or turbo trainer first. They'll give you all
the fun of changing a top or eating a roast dinner while riding, with none of the danger.

THE ZIP CODE

So, you hit the local big climb, aiming to claim the Strava KOM. Sweating and breathing hard, you ditch the high-cadence Froome tactic, opting for the ultimate pro climbing look instead. It's time to UNZIP!

Unzip your jersey to the naval and stamp on the pedals like Contador – showing everyone you mean business. Yes, it's an admission that you're working hard, but it also makes clear that you WON'T be beaten.

TOTAL PRO-GASM.

Don't forget, unzipping should reveal a good-luck talisman around your neck: something totally 70s Tom Jones. Be sure to get into a rhythm that makes the bling swing like a pendulum. Then, as you crest the climb, casually zip up your top once more – and bask in this moment of pro-looking glory.

OF THE TUBES

As a MAMIL, you'll know that cycling is gruelling at times. REALLY hard work is involved, and we're not just talking about shaving that tricky bit around your knee. That's why many pros write motivational quotes on their ride's top tube – to keep them going when the going gets tough!

Having a 'top tube list' of motivational quotes is a very pro thing to do. Looking down and seeing phrases such as
'SHUT UP LEGS'
'PAIN IS JUST WEAKNESS LEAVING YOUR BODY'
will help you squeeze every drop of power from your pins.

Why not add some fun to your top tube?
Nobody said you couldn't laugh while looking very pro.
'Mirror, mirror on the wall, who has the smoothest legs of all?'
'Shopping list: milk, eggs, beans and haemorrhoid cream.'

WARNING: Don't use permanent ink – what inspires you today may not do the job tomorrow.

SECTION THREE

POST-RIDE
LOOKING PRO OUT OF THE SADDLE

ESPRESSO YOURSELF

The friendly neighbourhood coffee shop is the natural habitat of the MAMIL. These cool cafés are the place to be for any pedaller with pretensions to appear pro. But how does a MAMIL (in the midst of so many others) rise above the rest? What must you do to show yourself as pro 'wheat' amongst so much Lycra-clad 'chaff'?

INSIDE THE COFFEE SHOP

Firstly, your drink has to be SMALL – espresso, macchiatto, flat white at a stretch. Like a pro, espresso is a drink of the bare essentials, carrying no extra baggage. (And never call it 'expresso', unless you want it in a hurry.)

Next, in your seat, it's important to unzip your top to underline how exhausted you are. Don't go too far, but other café-goers should catch a glimpse of the white of your bib.

In terms of conversation, make sure it's loud and repetitive. When referring to the distance covered, use this simple formula: actual mileage, add five and double it. You'll sound hugely pro.

OUTSIDE THE COFFEE SHOP

If you prefer your coffee al fresco,
it's important to follow these rules.

Ensure your group populates every chair.
Bikes should get a seat of their own – if the
ride is carbon give it two. Next, man-spread in
the extreme. Make sure you roll up your shorts
(to show off tan lines), then point your crotch
towards the sky. This is a VERY pro look.

Remember, one coffee post-ride
is NEVER enough. A coffee-shop
visit should be double the length
of the ride it succeeds.

Dedicated coffee-shop time is one of the best
ways to alert the masses to your newly acquired
pro-like status. So, to build your pro reputation,
don't be afraid to visit the coffee shop daily,
in full kit, even if you've not had time for a ride.

But, whatever you do, don't forget to bring
the bike with you. A MAMIL in Lycra
without a bike just looks silly.

CAP IT OFF

A - OFF THE BACK

B - REVERSE INVERTED FLIP

C - INVERTED FLIP

D - STRAIGHT FORWARD

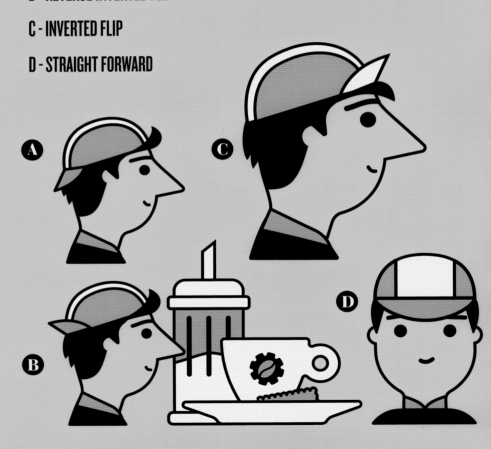

A cycling cap is a key part of any wannabe pro-rider's attire. Worn beneath a helmet it can be quirky and fun – and when left in place on your head during your post-ride coffee, it is a sure sign of pro-ness.

Wear it the right way to win the cap-game:

OFF THE BACK – you are one chilled-out, super-cool young pro.

REVERSE INVERTED FLIP – the ultimate post-ride look to match with coffee.

INVERTED FLIP – you're happy, you're pro, you've nailed a hardcore ride.

STRAIGHT FORWARD – average commuters just collapsed in your wake.

To be clear – other than on your bike, your local, boutique coffee shop is the ONLY place it's cool to wear your cap. Donning a cap to the supermarket or while picking the kids up from school may, to the untrained observer, seem quite a pro thing to do. It isn't.

Inside uber-stylish cafés, the usual rules of the cap-game do not apply. Lingering for a while in your pro headwear, sipping on an espresso, nibbling a croissant and popping a biscotti or two, is one of the pro-est things you can do.

AND THE REST (DAY)

Even God needed a day off, to chill out and reflect on what He'd done, and He hadn't even won the Strava KOM on his local killer climb!

Rest days, for any MAMIL who wants to seem pro, are essential.

Make sure you hit the sofa, taking the strain off the body that gave so much on your last ride. To get the full pro look, any couchtime must be done in full (clean) kit and documented by a series of selfies posted on social media – with captions that make it sound like you've come back from a war, not a social ride.

A diet of daytime TV is recommended. Be sure, however, to have some cycling standing by on another channel, so that you can flick over to La Vuelta or Tour of Britain should somebody barge into the room.

If you MUST leave the house, short-shorts that show off your tan-lines, along with sliders and white socks (at the correct length) are a must.

Remember, rest days are all about you. Use this time to perfect 'The Look', catch up on peloton hand signals and do some de-hairing.

25

GETTING SOCIAL

If a MAMIL goes for a ride and appears extremely pro, but doesn't put several pictures of it on social media, did it really happen?

There's no point in looking pro if nobody is around to see it. That's why the use of social media is essential for any rider with a desire to look more skilled than they actually are. Here are our key tips:

Edit your pictures. Screen out anything that shows how you really appear on a bike. Delete shots that show your tummy, moobs, bingo wings or cellulite. These images will not assist you in your quest to look pro.

Know your best angle. Disguise that double chin and take pics in low light so your black kit blends in with the surroundings and your figure disappears.

Communicate the struggle. If you experience rain or mud, it's essential to let the world know just how wet and/or muddy you are. Failing to provide your online fans with such images is bad form.

Go the distance. Any post about a ride should include a statement just slightly inflating the mileage you actually covered. Remember, it's vital to confer with co-riders and agree on what the distance will be – discrepancies down the line can be embarrassing.

Keep it clean. Avoid any shots where your 'luggage' may have fallen from behind the pad into a visible position. Nobody wants to see that. There's no point putting in so much effort to look pro if all anyone spots is how cold it was that day.

WE LEARNED?

So MAMIL, you now have zero excuses for looking anything other than utterly pro at all times.

It's really this simple:

- Slam the stem, shave to perfection and avoid sh*t kit.
- Get your socks right, tame a turbo, then lay it on thick with your look.
- On a ride, make it look easy – given the chance, an armpit glance.
- On corners, go low (not TOO low) and on straights never exclude the draft.
- Get to grips with cadence, know watt's what and master 'The Look'.
- In a chain-gang, flick off and give it all that with signals and shouts.
- A team car is great, if your bottle's sticky and there's a wheel to spare.
- Ride hands-free, unzip and climb – and try to avoid hospital time.
- Post ride, hit a coffee shop, man-spread and exaggerate your ride.
- Cap it off, get online and show the world just how pro you look.
- Above all, remember ...

LOOKING PRO ISN'T AS EASY AS RIDING A BIKE.

ABOUT THE AUTHORS

Illustrator and designer Spencer Wilson slipped into the life of a MAMIL after hanging up his football boots. He's fortunate to live in the cyclists' nirvana of Hertfordshire with his support crew – his wife Anna and two daughters. When he's not illustrating, you'll find Spencer wearing Lycra and riding his Cinelli around the Chilterns, or sipping an espresso in a bohemian coffee shop.

His other books include *The Modern MAMIL: A Cyclist's A–Z* and *H is for Hummus: A Modern Parent's ABC*, created with friend Joel Rickett.

 @spencerwilson8

 www.spencerwilson.co.uk

Writer and MAMIL Chris McGuire got into cycling because he'd bought all the Lycra and it would have looked weird if he didn't occasionally ride a bike. Based in Devon, Chris lives exclusively on a diet of chips and clotted cream. He used to work in telly, and now writes for several publications (including a couple with free gifts on the cover). Chris's dream is to be the world's most famous MAMIL – watch out Gordon Ramsay!

@McGuireski 🐦

A big thank you to Samantha Rigby at Ice House Books for some sterling work in the back room. Thanks also to Sue Bateman at Yellow House Art Licensing and Etta Saunders for their continued support.

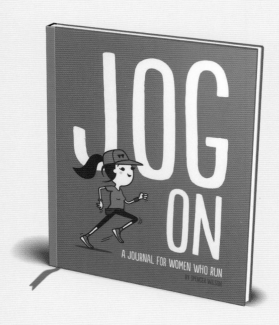